anythink

D0603840

anythink

A LOOK AT ANCIENT CIVILIZATIONS

ANCIENT EGYPT

BY DANIEL R. FAUST

Gareth Stevens
PUBLISHING

CRASHCOURSE

Please visit our website, www.garethstevens.com. For a free color catalog of all our high-quality books, call toll free 1-800-542-2595 or fax 1-877-542-2596.

Library of Congress Cataloging-in-Publication Data

Names: Faust, Daniel R., author.
Title: Ancient Egypt / Daniel R. Faust.
Description: New York : Gareth Stevens Publishing, 2019. | Series: A look at ancient civilizations | Includes index.
Identifiers: LCCN 2018015777| ISBN 9781538230053 (library bound) | ISBN 9781538231470 (pbk.) | ISBN 9781538233238 (6 pack)
Subjects: LCSH: Egypt--Civilization--Juvenile literature. | Egypt--History--To 332 B.C.--Juvenile literature. | Egypt--History--332-30 B.C.--Juvenile literature.
Classification: LCC DT61 .F297 2019 | DDC 932--dc23
LC record available at https://lccn.loc.gov/2018015777

First Edition

Published in 2019 by
Gareth Stevens Publishing
111 East 14th Street, Suite 349
New York, NY 10003

Copyright © 2019 Gareth Stevens Publishing

Designer: Reann Nye
Editor: Tayler Cole

Photo credits: Series art (writing background) mcherevan/Shutterstock.com, (map) Andrey_Kuzmin/Shutterstock.com; cover, p. 1 posztos/Shutterstock.com; p. 5 Peter Hermes Furian/Shutterstock.com; p. 7 Tanatat pongphibool ,thailand/Moment/Getty Images; p. 9 PHAS/Universal Images Group/Getty Images; p. 11 Bettmann/Getty Images; p. 13 Waj/Shutterstock.com; p. 15 Dean Mouhtaropoulos/Getty Images News/Getty Images; p. 17 Fedor Selivanov/Shutterstock.com; p. 19 Marcin Sylwia Ciesielski/Shutterstock.com; p. 21 Heritage Images/Hulton Archive/Getty Images; p. 23 Anton_Ivanov/Shutterstock.com; p. 25 Radiokafka/Shutterstock.com; p. 27 Leonid Andronov/Shutterstock.com; p. 29 Ancientrome.ru/PericlesofAthens/Wikipedia.org.

Printed in the United States of America

CPSIA compliance information: Batch #CW19GS: For further information contact Gareth Stevens, New York, New York at 1-800-542-2595.

CONTENTS

Words in the glossary appear in **bold** type the first time they are used in the text.

A RIVER IN EGYPT

At about 4,132 miles (6,650 km) long, the Nile River in Egypt is one of the world's longest rivers. It starts in east central Africa and then flows into the Mediterranean Sea. The first people in Egypt settled along the Nile River.

Make The Grade

Each year from July through September, the Nile River flooded the nearby land. These floods were dangerous, but they also helped turn desert into farmland along the riverbanks.

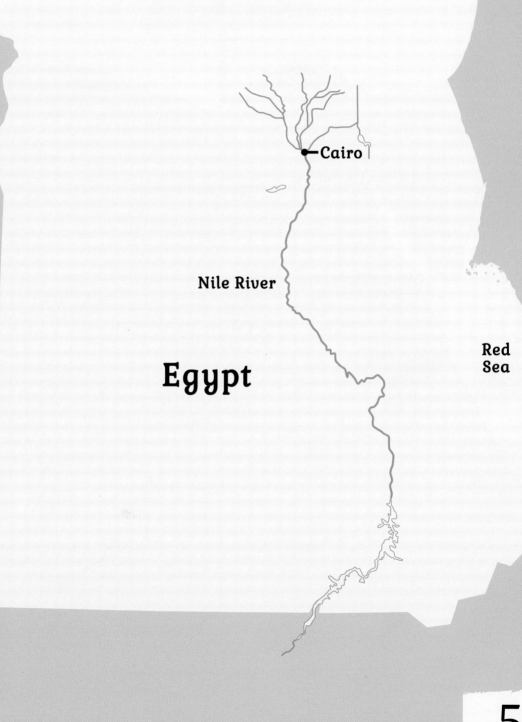

Mediterranean Sea

Cairo

Nile River

Egypt

Red
Sea

5

Early Egyptians used the rich soil along the Nile's riverbanks to grow grain and raise pigs, sheep, and cattle. Around 4000 BC, neighboring villages throughout Egypt began joining together to form **provinces** called nomes.

Make The Grade

The Nile River was also used for moving people and goods from one place to another. A plant called papyrus was used to make small boats, which were floated down the river.

TWO EGYPTS BECOME ONE

Over time, the Egyptian civilization grew into two kingdoms. Lower Egypt was located in the river **delta** of the north. Upper Egypt was located in the drier valley to the south.

Make The Grade

The kings of Upper Egypt wore a white crown. The kings of Lower Egypt wore a red crown. When the two lands later **united**, a double crown was created that was both red and white.

8

pschent
double crown

9

In 3100 BC, the kingdoms of Upper and Lower Egypt were united by Menes. Menes, sometimes also called Narmer, was a king from Upper Egypt. Under his leadership, Egypt became a single, powerful nation. Menes became Egypt's first pharaoh, or king.

Menes

Make The Grade

Though the lands were united, Egyptians still called the
new kingdom the "two lands." Soon this land became
simply known as Egypt.

THE OLD KINGDOM

Egyptian history is divided, or split, into three periods called kingdoms. The first period is called the Old Kingdom, and it lasted from 2575 BC until 2130 BC. During the Old Kingdom, the Egyptians built large tombs, or burial rooms, and monuments to honor the pharaohs.

Make The Grade

Because of the monuments built during this time, the Old Kingdom is also called the "pyramid age." The Old Kingdom pharaohs are called "pyramid builders."

GODS AND PHARAOHS

Ancient Egyptian **religion** was polytheistic, which meant the people believed in more than one god. Egyptians thought these gods created and controlled their world. Pharaohs were also **worshipped** because they were a **connection** between the gods and humans.

Make The Grade

People thought pharaohs were all-powerful and all-knowing. When a pharaoh died, he became **divine** and was worshipped like a god.

15

HIEROGLYPHICS

Ancient Egyptians used a form of writing called hieroglyphics. Hieroglyphics used pictures or **symbols** to stand for words, sounds, and ideas. Much of the information historians have about ancient Egypt comes from hieroglyphics that were painted on walls or carved into stone.

Make The Grade

We can read hieroglyphics thanks to the Rosetta Stone, a stone tablet containing the same text written three different ways: in hieroglyphics, demotic writing, and in classic Greek.

THE MIDDLE KINGDOM

The Middle Kingdom lasted from 1938 BC until 1630 BC. The Middle Kingdom was a time of growth. Pharaohs wanted to spread their power into nearby lands. During this time, Egypt also traded with the Minoan civilization in Greece.

Make The Grade

During the Middle Kingdom, more soldiers joined the military and the pharaohs built a series of forts to keep Egypt safe from **invaders**.

THE NEW KINGDOM

Around 1630 BC, Egypt was invaded by the Hyksos, a group of people from western Asia. The Hyksos ruled for about 100 years before being forced out of Egypt. The New Kingdom, which followed, lasted from 1539 BC until 1075 BC.

Make The Grade

Women had many freedoms in ancient Egypt. They could own land and run businesses. Some women could even be pharaoh! Queen Hatshepsut ruled as pharaoh during the New Kingdom.

21

The New Kingdom was a period of great **wealth**, growth, and **empire** building. Egypt's military successfully pushed into Syria, Nubia, and lands found around the Mediterranean Sea. As Egypt's population grew, more people moved to the cities. There, art and religion became more popular.

Make The Grade

During the New Kingdom, pharaohs built giant **statues** and buildings. One pharaoh, Ramses II, even built his own city called Pi-Ramesse.

EGYPT ON THE DECLINE

After spending all its money on building projects and the military, Egypt was once again weakened. Invaders began taking over, and Egypt lost much of the land it had conquered, or took over, during the New Kingdom. In 525 BC, the Persian Empire conquered Egypt.

Make The Grade

During the Late period (664–332 BC), animal worship became a more important part of Egyptian religion. Many kinds of animals were made into mummies around this time.

CONQUEST OF EGYPT

In 332 BC, Alexander the Great conquered Egypt as he created the largest empire of his time. He left his mark on Egypt by creating a new city called Alexandria. Alexandria was home to the famous Library of Alexandria, a center of great learning.

Make The Grade

After Alexander's death, the city of Alexandria became the new capital of Egypt and an important place for trade.

CLEOPATRA AND THE ROMANS

Cleopatra was the last pharaoh of Egypt before it fell to the Roman Empire. Egypt's small army was too weak to fight off invaders. Egypt was part of the Roman Empire from 30 BC until about AD 395 when the Roman Empire was divided.

Cleopatra

Make The Grade

The ancient Egyptian civilization lasted for almost 3,000 years.
When the Roman Empire split in two in the late 4th century,
many of the ancient Egyptian ways of life were lost.

29

TIMELINE OF ANCIENT EGYPT

c. 5000 BC
Farms form along the Nile River.

3100 BC
Upper Egypt and Lower Egypt are united into a single kingdom.

2575–2130 BC
The Old Kingdom.

1938–1630 BC
The Middle Kingdom.

1539–1075 BC
The New Kingdom.

525 BC
Persian Empire conquers Egypt.

332 BC
Alexander the Great conquers Egypt and founds the city of Alexandria.

30 BC
Egypt falls to the Roman Empire.

GLOSSARY

connection: something that joins two or more things

delta: land shaped like a triangle at the mouth of a river

divine: relating to or coming from a god

empire: a large area of land under the control of a single ruler

invader: someone who enters a place to take it over

province: an area of a country

religion: a belief in and way of honoring a god or gods

statue: a figure, usually of a person or animal, that is made from stone or metal

symbol: a picture, shape, or object that stands for something else

unite: to cause two or more things to join together and become one thing

wealth: the value of all the money, land, and belongings that someone or something has

worship: to honor as a god

FOR MORE INFORMATION

BOOKS

Hart, George. *Ancient Egypt*. New York, NY: DK Publishing, 2014.

Randolph, Joanne. *The Myths and Legends of Ancient Egypt and Africa*. New York, NY: Cavendish Square, 2018.

WEBSITE

10 Facts About Ancient Egypt
www.natgeokids.com/uk/discover/history/egypt/ten-facts-about-ancient-egypt
Learn more about ancient Egypt and what Egypt is like today.

INDEX